Spirit:

Cocktail Name:

Type:

Ingredients:

Garnish:

Mixing Method:

Glass:

Additional Notes:

In Ireland, there's a tradition known as The 12 Pubs of Christmas. You go to 12 different pubs in one night, having a drink in each. Because nothing says festive like a liver workout!

Spirit:
Cocktail Name:
Type:

Ingredients:

Garnish:

Mixing Method:

Glass:

Additional Notes:

In Finland, 'kalsarikannit'
means to get drunk alone at
home in your underpants.
Because sometimes, pants are
just too much effortr

Spirit:
Cocktail Name:
Type:

Ingredients:

Garnish:

Mixing Method:

Glass:

Additional Notes:

Millions of liters of beer that expired in Australia amid the coronavirus pandemic have been converted into renewable energy, powering up to 1,200 homes per week. Talk about a buzz-worthy solution!

Spirit:

Cocktail Name:

Type:

Ingredients:

Garnish:

Mixing Method:

Glass:

Additional Notes:

Mixing alcohol with diet mixers gets you 18% more drunk than with full-fat mixers because your body doesn't recognize aspartame as food. So, you get drunk quicker and cheaper!

Diet Mixer
Diet Mixer
Full-Fat
Diet Mixer
Full-Fat
Mixer
VEL EOT CLET
Full-Fat Fat Mixer
Full-Fat Mixer

Spirit:

Cocktail Name:

Type:

Ingredients:

Garnish:

Mixing Method:

Glass:

Additional Notes:

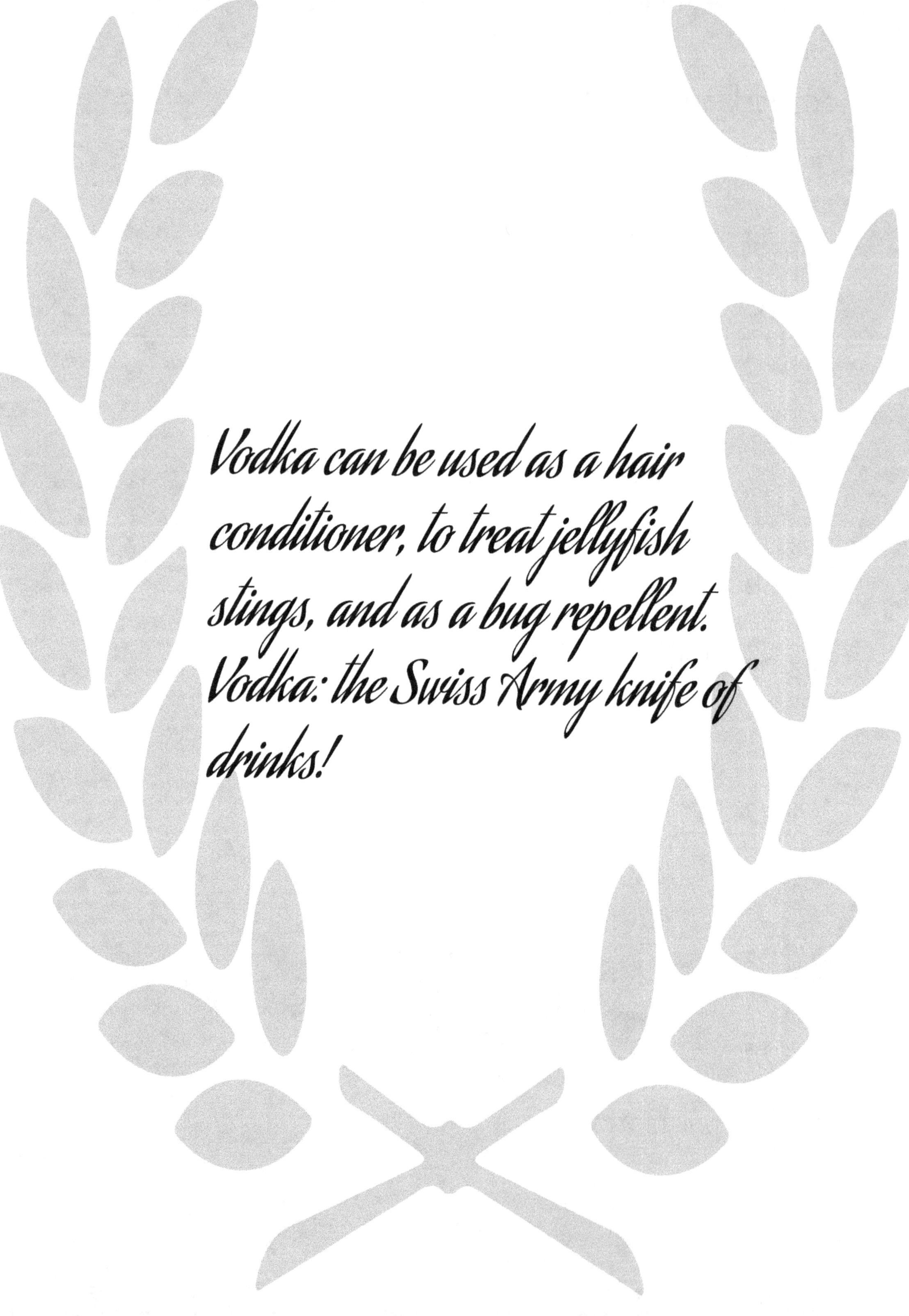

Vodka can be used as a hair conditioner, to treat jellyfish stings, and as a bug repellent. Vodka: the Swiss Army knife of drinks!

VOKA
VODKA

Spirit:

Cocktail Name:

Type:

Ingredients:

Garnish:

Mixing Method:

Glass:

Additional Notes:

Every day, a winery in Spain sets out a glass of sherry and a tiny ladder for the mice living in the cellars. Legend has it that a worker found a mouse sipping from his wine glass and, feeling bad that the mouse couldn't indulge as much as he could, got it a tiny glass for its own use. Talk about a high-class rodent!

Spirit:

Cocktail Name:

Type:

Ingredients:

Garnish:

Mixing Method:

Glass:

Additional Notes:

Alcohol doesn't cause you to forget what happened. Your brain just stops forming new memories when you've had too much to drink. So, technically, it's not your fault you forgot your keys in the fridge.

Spirit:

Cocktail Name:

Type:

Ingredients:

Garnish:

Mixing Method:

Glass:

Additional Notes:

Wisconsin has the same number of bars as California, despite a population that's 85% smaller. That's one bar for every 1,862 residents compared to California's one for every 11,962. Clearly, Wisconsin takes their socializing seriously!

Spirit:

Cocktail Name:

Type:

Ingredients:

Garnish:

Mixing Method:

Glass:

Additional Notes:

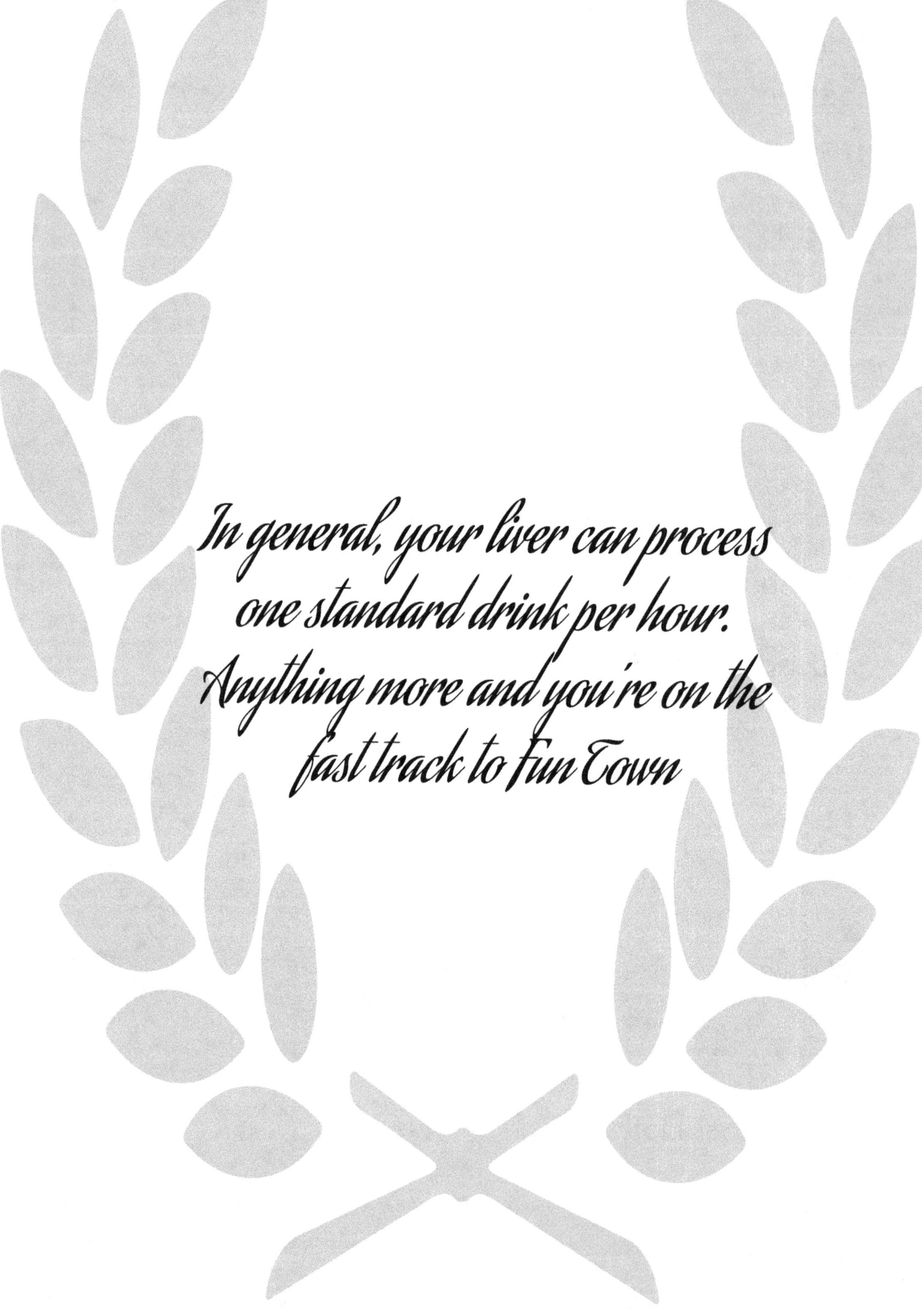
In general, your liver can process
one standard drink per hour.
Anything more and you're on the
fast track to Fun Town

Fun Town.

Spirit:

Cocktail Name:

Type:

Ingredients:

Garnish:

Mixing Method:

Glass:

Additional Notes:

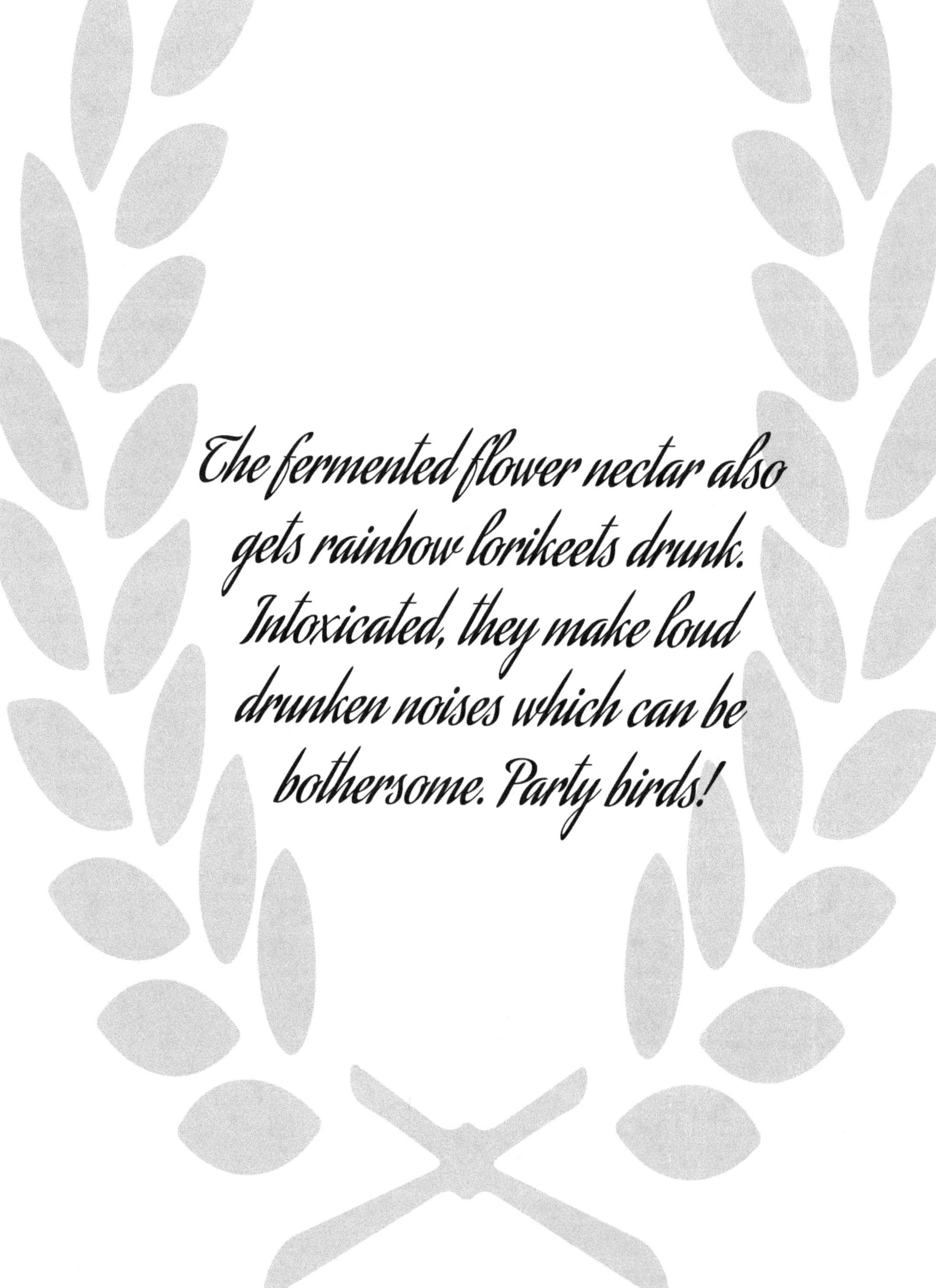
The fermented flower nectar also gets rainbow lorikeets drunk. Intoxicated, they make loud drunken noises which can be bothersome. Party birds!

Spirit:

Cocktail Name:

Type:

Ingredients:

Garnish:

Mixing Method:

Glass:

Additional Notes:

In Australia, when it gets hot, the nectar in some flowers ferments and turns into alcohol. Bees that get drunk from the nectar are kept out of the hive by 'bouncer' bees to prevent alcoholic honey. Party poopers!

Spirit:

Cocktail Name:

Type:

Ingredients:

Garnish:

Mixing Method:

Glass:

Additional Notes:

Saint Arnold of Soissons is the Catholic Saint of Beer. He saved lives by urging people to drink beer instead of water during the plague. Cheers to Arnold!

Water

Spirit:

Cocktail Name:

Type:

Ingredients:

Garnish:

Mixing Method:

Glass:

Additional Notes:

The most expensive beer in the US is Samuel Adams' Utopia, costing $210 per bottle and with a 28% ABV. It's banned in 15 states, proving not everyone can handle the utopia.

TODHOI APRV
SHANT BRINGS
280
ABV
$10
ABV
BEER

Spirit:
Cocktail Name:
Type:

Ingredients:

Garnish:

Mixing Method:

Glass:

Additional Notes:

In the 1800s, Americans drank an average of 90 bottles of whiskey per year because whiskey was cheaper than water. Cheers to historical hydration!

Spirit:

Cocktail Name:

Type:

Ingredients:

Garnish:

Mixing Method:

Glass:

Additional Notes:

Cenosillicaphobia is the fear of an empty beer glass. Now that's a real problem!

Spirit:

Cocktail Name:

Type:

Ingredients:

Garnish:

Mixing Method:

Glass:

Additional Notes:

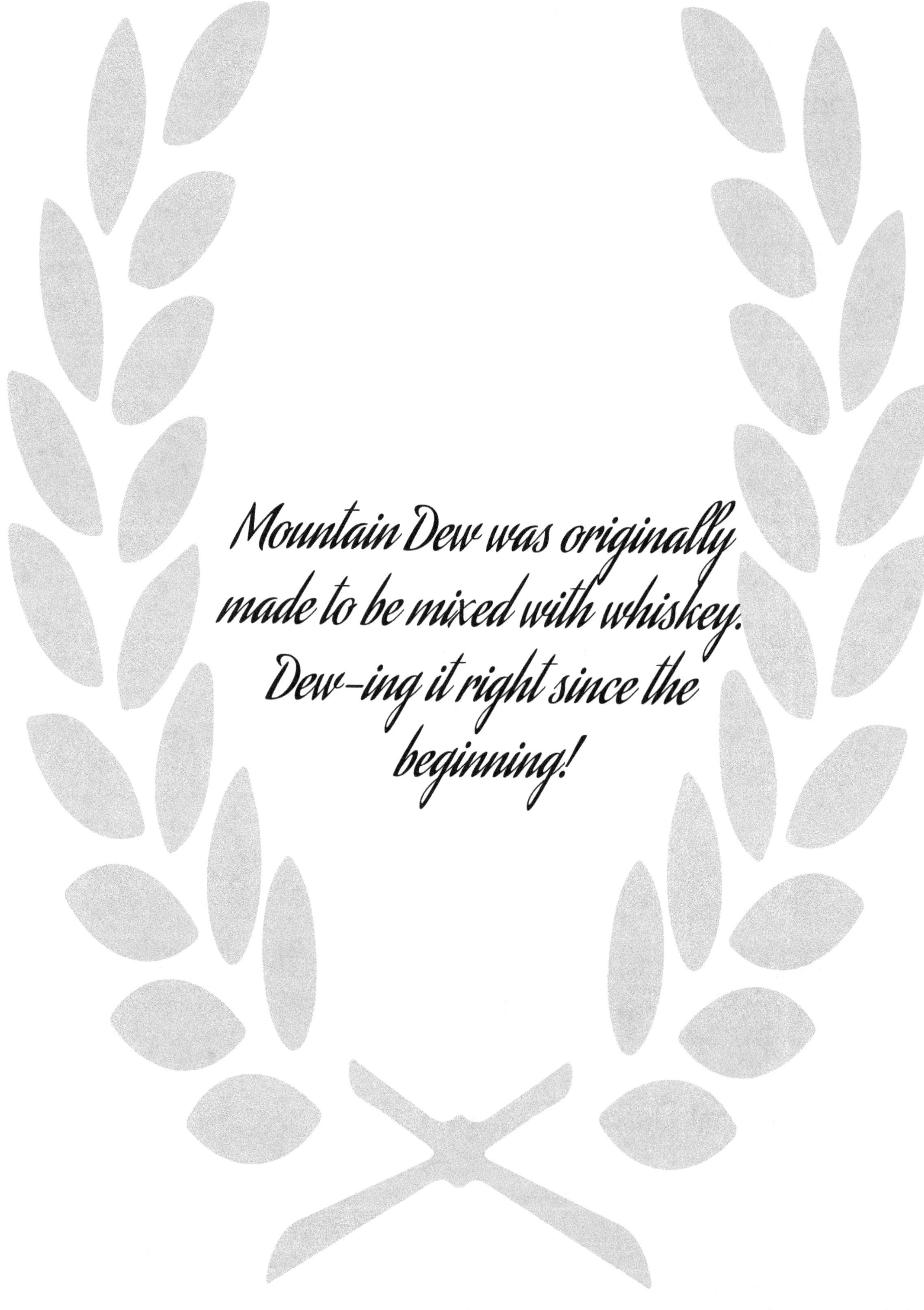
Mountain Dew was originally
made to be mixed with whiskey.
Dew-ing it right since the
beginning!

Spirit:

Cocktail Name:

Type:

Ingredients:

Garnish:

Mixing Method:

Glass:

Additional Notes:

A banana milkshake sweetened with honey is one of the best ways to cure a hangover. The banana calms the stomach, and the honey builds up blood sugar levels. Plus, it's delicious!

Spirit:

Cocktail Name:

Type:

Ingredients:

Garnish:

Mixing Method:

Glass:

Additional Notes:

India consumes half the world's whiskey, but the French drink the most per person at 2.15 liters annually. Cheers to both!

Spirit:

Cocktail Name:

Type:

Ingredients:

Garnish:

Mixing Method:

Glass:

Additional Notes:

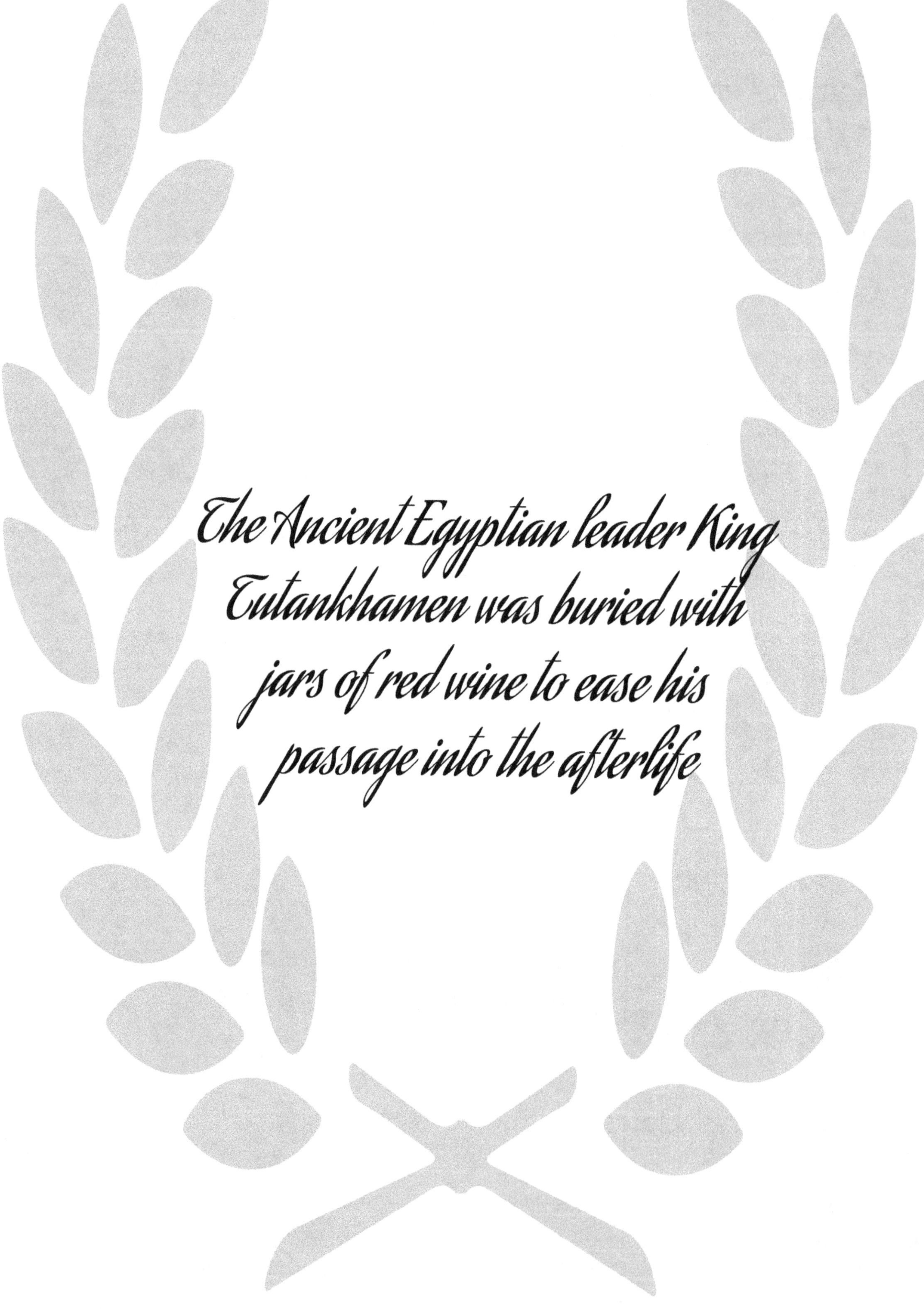
The Ancient Egyptian leader King Tutankhamen was buried with jars of red wine to ease his passage into the afterlife

Spirit:

Cocktail Name:

Type:

Ingredients:

Garnish:

Mixing Method:

Glass:

Additional Notes:

Drinking a ton of beer can make you smarter! Studies show large amounts of hops can improve cognitive function. Downside: you'd need to drink 3,520 pints in a day. So, you'll be the smartest... but also the deadest person ever.

Spirit:

Cocktail Name:

Type:

Ingredients:

Garnish:

Mixing Method:

Glass:

Additional Notes:

'Wine windows' were used by vintners in Tuscany during the 1630s Bubonic plague. These allowed merchants to pass wine to customers without contact. They're making a comeback due to coronavirus. Some things never change!

Spirit:

Cocktail Name:

Type:

Ingredients:

Garnish:

Mixing Method:

Glass:

Additional Notes:

Peter the Great created The Council of Drunken Fools, whose job was to drink and party. Maybe he should be known as Peter the Party Animal!

Spirit:

Cocktail Name:

Type:

Ingredients:

Garnish:

Mixing Method:

Glass:

Additional Notes:

An attempt to set the Guinness World Record for the most expensive cocktail was thwarted when a customer dropped a $77,000 bottle of Cognac. Oops.

Spirit:

Cocktail Name:

Type:

Ingredients:

Garnish:

Mixing Method:

Glass:

Additional Notes:

Fruit flies drink alcohol when
they're sexually frustrated.
Because even fruit flies need a
drink after a rough day.

uit
ght Out.
Fly Brew
Night Out.
Fly's NigFt's
Brut Fly Lounge

Spirit:
Cocktail Name:
Type:

Ingredients:

Garnish:

Mixing Method:

Glass:

Additional Notes:

Sailors used to measure rum proof by mixing it with gunpowder and igniting it. Only the rum that exploded had the right alcohol concentration. This is why you don't mess with sailors or their rum.

Rum Testing
Proof of Nimin cengs of Strength

Spirit:

Cocktail Name:

Type:

Ingredients:

Garnish:

Mixing Method:

Glass:

Additional Notes:

Alcohol increases creativity by reducing executive function and boosting imagination. This is why some of your best ideas happen at the bottom of a wine glass.

Spirit:

Cocktail Name:

Type:

Ingredients:

Garnish:

Mixing Method:

Glass:

Additional Notes:

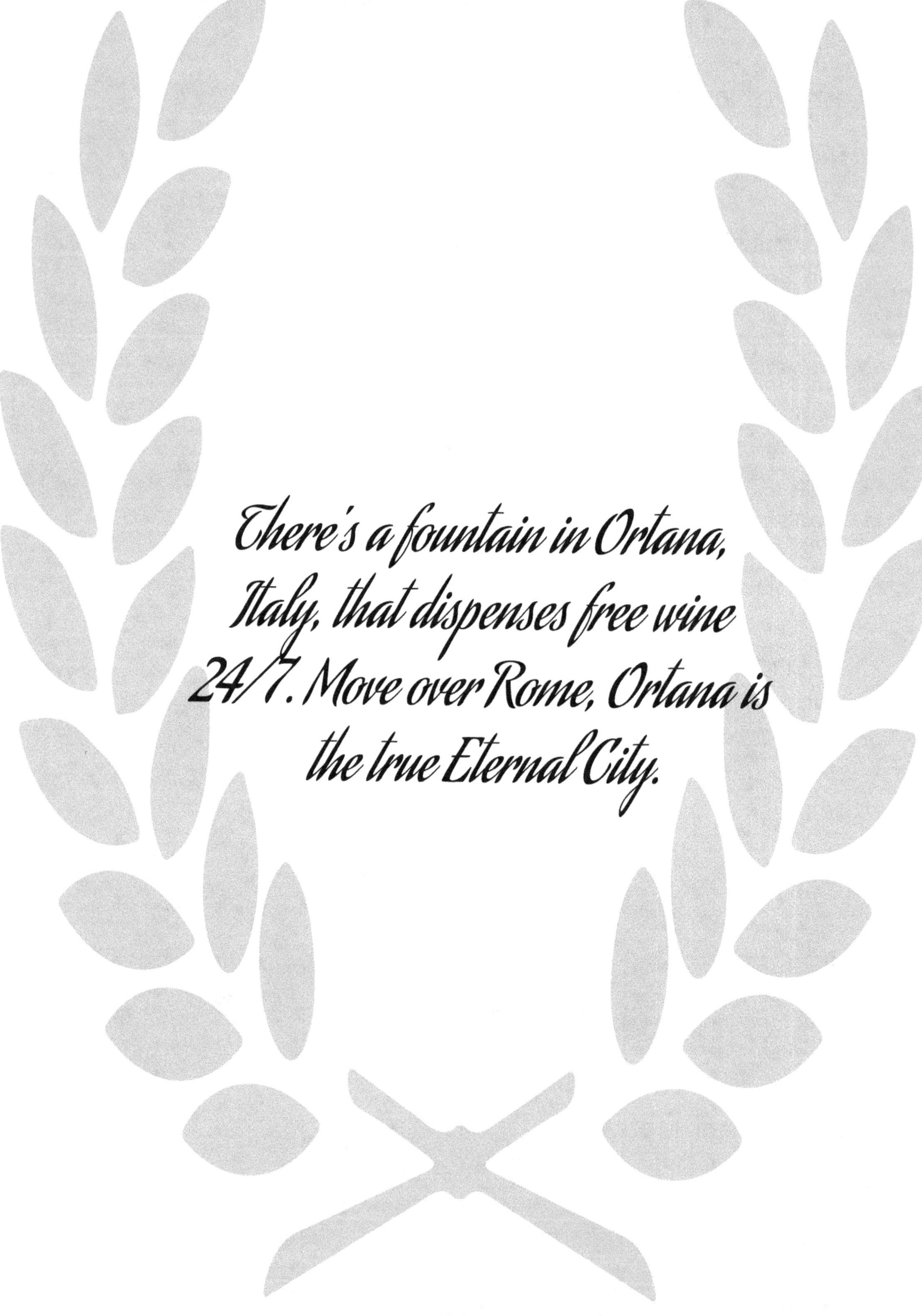

There's a fountain in Ortana, Italy, that dispenses free wine 24/7. Move over Rome, Ortana is the true Eternal City.

Spirit:

Cocktail Name:

Type:

Ingredients:

Garnish:

Mixing Method:

Glass:

Additional Notes:

Researchers concluded there are four types of drunks: The Hemingway (stays the same), The Mary Poppins (sweeter and more outgoing), The Nutty Professor (uninhibited attention-seeker), and Mr. Hyde (hostile). Which one are you?

Spirit:

Cocktail Name:

Type:

Ingredients:

Garnish:

Mixing Method:

Glass:

Additional Notes:

Russia banned vodka sales during World War I, and the government immediately lost a third of its income. Lesson learned: never come between Russians and their vodka.

Vodka.
Vodka Ban.

Spirit:

Cocktail Name:

Type:

Ingredients:

Garnish:

Mixing Method:

Glass:

Additional Notes:

'Butt' is a medieval unit of measurement for wine. A butt load of wine is 129 gallons. Now you know where the phrase comes from!

BUTT